Before Tying the Knot

Questions couples must ask each other __Before__ they marry!

ROBERTA CAVA

Published by Cava Consulting

info@dealingwithdifficultpeople.info

www.dealingwithdifficultpeople.info

National Library of Australia

Cataloguing-in-publication data:

Cava, Roberta

Before tying the knot
Questions couples must ask
each other Before they marry

ISBN 978-0-9923579-9-3

BOOKS BY ROBERTA CAVA

Non-Fiction

Dealing with Difficult People
(21 publishers – in 16 languages)
Dealing with Difficult Situations – at Work and at Home
Dealing with Difficult Spouses and Children
Dealing with Difficult Relatives and In-Laws
Dealing with Domestic Violence and Child Abuse
Dealing with School Bullying
Dealing with Workplace Bullying
Retirement Village Bullies
Keeping Our Children Safe
What am I going to do with the rest of my life?
Before tying the knot – Questions couples Must ask each other
Before they marry!
How Women can advance in business
Survival Skills for Supervisors and Managers
Human Resources at its Best!
Human Resources Policies and Procedures - Australia
Employee Handbook
Easy Come – Hard to go – The Art of Hiring, Disciplining and
Firing Employees
Time and Stress – Today's silent killers
Take Command of your Future – Make things Happen
Belly Laughs for All! – Volumes 1 to 4
Wisdom of the World! The happy, sad and wise things in life!

Fiction

That Something Special
Something Missing
Trilogy: Life Gets Complicated
Life Goes On
Life Gets Better

Before Tying the Knot!

Questions couples Must ask Before they marry!

Table of Contents

* Broom's "To Do" List
* Tips for Choosing the Perfect Wedding Gown
* Wedding Budget Check-List
* Who pays for what?
* Wedding Toasts
* Dress Codes Men/Women
* Marriage Contracts/Pre-nuptial Agreements
* The Matrimonial Home
* Cohabitation Agreements

HOW TO USE

This pre-marital workbook is for couples who might not have a strong religious affiliation, or don't have access to pre-marital counselling. It is a tool for increasing a couple's knowledge of how each partner thinks and believes about hundreds of every-day preferences. (It can also be used by couples that are thinking of living together.)

Chapter One is for her - Chapter Two is for him. There are ten groups of questions, and each chapter contains over 200 questions. So neither of you will be influenced by your partner's answers, it's important that you complete the questions in the chapters **before** you discuss any of the questions together.

By completing the questions individually first, the likelihood of one partner skipping over crucial issues will be eliminated. After you've completed the chapters, you and your partner may decide to discuss only one group of questions at a time.

I'm sure you'll find many areas where you do not agree - areas that you had never thought of discussing. Best wishes for a successful wedding and a long and happy marriage!

Don't marry a person that you know you can live with.
Only marry someone that you cannot live without!

INTRODUCTION

It takes most of us many years of training to prepare for our careers, but how much training have you taken to prepare yourself for two of the most important events in your life - choosing a mate and having a family? And how do you really know whether you're in love? What signs show you that "this is the one for me?"

When a couple marry, they leave behind thinking only for and of themselves, and change most aspects of their existing lives. Now they face life together, united by love, but remaining two distinct individuals. As a couple, you'll confide in each other, depend upon each other, have new responsibilities to each other, create new family ties, develop a stable home, and bring forth the signs of your love - your children.

The main ingredient for a successful marriage, is giving unquestionable trust and love to each other. This means not only sharing ideas, but being open and honest with each other. Couples accomplish this by being in touch with what's really going on inside themselves and being willing to share those feelings with each other. This eliminates manipulation, and results in honest, DIRECT communication.

There are many questions a couple should ask themselves before they take the big step into marriage. Unfortunately, if couples don't have a strong religious affiliation, they often run into a dead end when trying to find someone who will offer pre-marital counselling. Couples are often in for a big surprise, if they neglect to ask each other crucial questions about what they expect out of their relationship.

You can prepare for your marriage by following these steps:

a) Each partner privately answers the questions, which takes one to two hours to complete. Really put some thought to each question. Don't be tempted to answer the way you think your partner would answer. You'll be able to compromise later, but right now these must be YOUR answers!

b) Then meet to discuss how you answered every question. This part will likely take another two or three hours to complete.

c) Then discuss areas of conflict, and make compromises as required.

This process takes time, but it's time well spent. Some might find the answers to questions makes them decide *against* "tying the knot," but it's better to know now, before promising a lifetime commitment, and ending up in divorce court.

You must be prepared to make a time commitment to make this work!

CHAPTER 1

PRE-MARITAL QUESTIONS

HERS

Answer the following questions when you have time to really consider what you want to answer. Do **NOT** complete your questions together otherwise you will influence each other's answers.

Be sure to complete these questions **before** getting married:

IS IT "TRUE LOVE?"

There are many signs that point to true love. Here are some of them - decide what you would answer. Just put a **tick mark** next to those you agree with, and an **"X"** next to the ones you don't agree with.

1. When I consider the person I'd prefer be with - it's with him.
2. I find I've quit examining and sizing up other men as potential mates.
3. I'm quite content with him as he is. I wouldn't change any of his major characteristics.
4. I respect his talents and abilities.
5. He doesn't try to change how I am or things I believe in.
6. I find him to be a very interesting person.
7. I respect and trust him.
8. I feel we could be best friends for life.
9. This is the strongest relationship in my life.
10. I miss him when we're not together.
11. I always think of him - he's always present with me wherever I go, if only in spirit.

12. I feel excitement when we're together.

13. I have a special feeling about him that I don't feel with anyone else.

14. We don't have to talk to be companionable.

15. We both want to surprise each other with little things we know will please the other.

16. We have a strong physical attraction, love touching, and ache for each other when we're apart.

17. When we're together, I'm the happiest I can remember.

18. We love planning activities we can do together.

19. We're very protective of the other's well-being and are ready to defend each other.

20. We have a great deal of influence over each other.

21. We're on the same wave-length and often know what the other is thinking.

22. I would never deceive or be unfaithful to him.

23. We like each other's friends.

24. We enjoy doing many of the same activities.

25. We feel we could grow old happily with each other.

26. We're capable of being very intimate – there are no barriers between us. We're freely able to tell each other how we feel and discuss situations that bother us.

27. I feel he had good role models. If he didn't, he's had counselling to make sure the cycle doesn't repeat itself.

28. We're not afraid to be vulnerable to each other. We trust each other not to hurt the other.

29. We're not together simply because we don't want to be alone.

30. We both want a partner, not because we need one, but because we want one.

31. We are fulfilled, and happy with ourselves as people.

32. We're there to help celebrate each other's good days and cheer and support each other through bad days.

33. We stand by each other when we're sick, depressed or vulnerable to others.

34. We encourage each other to have other lives with our families and friends.

35. We are not possessive or jealous when we're in mixed company. Our trust for each other allows us to know the other will do the right thing.

36. We do not depend on each other to give each other a good day - we're able to do that for ourselves.

37. There are no topics or issues we can't or won't discuss.

PRE-MARITAL QUESTIONS

Now that you've established that you **are** in love, answer the following as honestly as possible. Take your time to seriously consider each question:

OUR WEDDING

1. a) What kind of wedding will we have – large, small, house of worship, celebrant, Justice of the Peace?

   b) What kind of service will we have?

   c) Who will be paying for which marriage expenses?

   d) Where will we hold our wedding (what city, town, which house of worship)?

   e) Where will the reception be held?

f) How many people will we invite? Young children too?

g) Will we both invite an equal number of guests? Yes / No

h) If parents divorced - any problems anticipated? Describe:

i) Who will stand up for us? Him? Me?

j) Who will give me away?

k) Where and how will we spend our honeymoon?

l) Will we have an engagement party? Yes / No

m) Do an engagement announcement? Yes / No

n) What will our wedding invitations say?

2. a) Will I be keeping my maiden name or will I use his name?

   b) At home? At work?

AT HOME:

1. a) Where will we live: in an apartment, home, with family?

   b) Which city or town?

2. a) What major possessions will I bring into our home?

   b) What items do I feel we need to buy for our home?

   c) How much money will we need for this?

3. Do I have a car? Yes / No. How much is owing on it?

4. Should we both have an equal say in all family decisions?

   Yes/No. Explain:

5. How much housework would each of us do? He? Me?

6. a) How often do I like to eat out?

   b) Do I like to cook? Yes/ No.

   c) What are my favourite foods?

   d) What foods do I hate/won't eat?

7. Do I like pets? Do I expect to have one or more in my home? Explain:

CHILDREN:

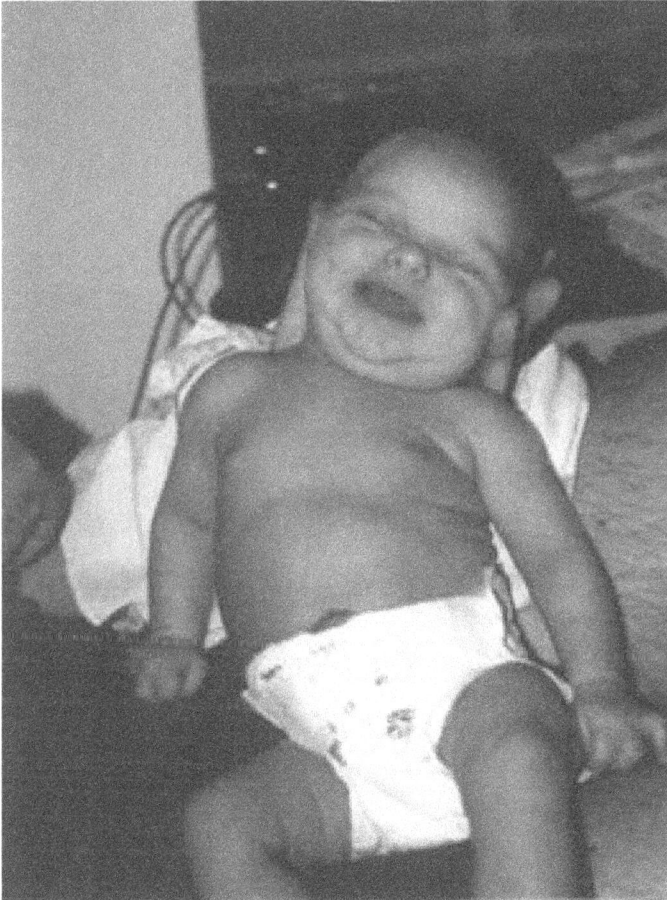

1. Am I able to have children? If not, why not?
2. a) How do I feel about mothers working after they have
    children?

   b) If they stay at home - for how long?
3. a) What are my views on birth control?

   b) What method of birth control would I want to use?

c) What are my views on abortion?

d) Have I ever had an abortion? Yes/ No. If yes,
     explain:

4. a) How many children do I want? Boys? Girls?

   b) When would I like to start a family?

   c) If a child were to arrive before that time, how would
      I feel?

   d) If our child was born with a deformity, a disability
      or mentally challenged, would I accept the child?
      Yes / No.

   e) Would I love this child less? Yes / No.

   f) What if we couldn't have our own children, would I
      want to adopt? Yes / No.

   g) Of our own culture? Other?

   h) Would I treat an adopted child as if it were mine?
      Yes /No.

5. a) How much time am I willing to give to the actual
      upbringing of our children?

   b) Would I be willing to get up at night to care for our
      children?

   c) What duties would I not be willing to do for our
      children?

6. a) Describe what I think my parenting style would be.

   b) Who should discipline our children? He? Me? Both?

FINANCES:

1. How much money will we have to live on? His salary? Mine?

2. Would I describe myself as: Frugal? Spend freely?

3. How do I spend my money?

4. What percentage/amount of our budget should we spend on fun?

5. a) Name the credit cards I use regularly:

   b) What amount of money do I owe now (credit cards, loans, etc)? Give details on repayment arrangements.

   c) How do I use my credit cards now?

   d) How will I use credit in the future?

6. a) Will we keep a budget? Yes / No.

   b) Do I know how to keep a budget? Yes / No.

c) Who will manage our money? I manage? He manage? We'll manage together? How will we do this?

7. a) How do I feel we should handle our paycheques and bills?

b) Should we have: joint? Separate? Or both? Bank accounts?

c) How much money will each of us have to spend on ourselves each week? He? Me? Who will decide this?

MY HISTORY:

1. Have I been married before? Explain.

2. a) Have I ever had children? Explain.

   b) What part will they play in our lives?

3. a) Do I have any disabilities he doesn't know about?
      Yes /No. If yes: explain:

   b) Do I take medication for any chronic illness? Yes /
      No. If yes: explain:

   c) Do I snore? Yes / No

   d) How is my general health?

      Physical?

      Emotional?

      Mental?

      Explain:

e) Do I like to be busy? Prefer a less-hectic lifestyle?

4. Do I have an under- or overweight problem? Yes / No.

5. a) How do I get along with my parents?

   b) My brothers?

   c) My sisters?

   d) Other relatives?

   e) Explain:

6. How often would we visit my family – they visit us? Explain:

7. What kind of childhood did I have? Explain:

8. a) Did I come from a dysfunctional home? Explain.

   b) If so, did I obtain counselling? Yes / No.

9. Have I ever had a criminal record? Yes /No. Explain:

10. Do I like to gamble? Yes / No. If excessive, explain:

11. Amount of alcohol consumed in a week? Explain. Any drug dependency? Explain:

12. What are my views on: Having guns in our home? Capital punishment?

13. a) What is my driving record? Explain if there have been difficulties:

    b) Do I ever drink and drive or drive unsafely? Yes / No.

14. Am I going to continue smoking (if applicable)? Yes / No.

15. Will we allow smoking in our home or vehicles? Yes / No.

MY PERSONALITY:

1. Am I a: neat? messy? person?

2. Am I a: morning? night? person?

3. Describe my average energy level - high? Medium? Low?

4. How do I manage time? Always early? Late? Do I procrastinate?

5. Am I a pack-rat? Dispose of unnecessary clutter?

6. Do I like to pull practical jokes? Have I hurt others' feelings?

7. Do I feel comfortable discussing my innermost feelings? Yes / No. Explain:

8. How important to me is the expression of affection? Explain:

9. Am I a romantic person (flowers, love notes, etc.)? Yes /No.

10. Do I like to be touched? Yes / No. In public? Only where there's privacy?

11. Do I prefer: being with friends? Being alone? With family members?

12. How often would I like to entertain? Explain: His friends? My friends?

13. Do I dislike any of his friends? Yes / No. Explain:

14. a) How do I view his having friends of the opposite sex?

   b) Would I object if he saw other women alone? Yes / No.

c) Would I describe myself as a jealous person? Yes / No.

d) If yes, how do I deal with jealousy?

15. When we're married, how much time will I spend with "the girls?"

16. How do I like to spend my leisure time?

17. How much time do I spend on hobbies or volunteer work?

18. Would I describe myself as a workaholic? Yes / No. Explain:

19. a) Describe my basic personality type: Extrovert? Introvert?

    b) Do I like to have music or the radio playing or do I like it best when it's quiet?

20. a) Do I feel comfortable giving/receiving compliments? Yes / No.

    b) Do I need reassurance from the important people in my life? Yes? Sometimes? No?

21. a) Describe my moods - steady, erratic, up one minute – down the next?

    b) How do I deal with and relieve stress? Explain:

    c) When I'm troubled, do I share my problems? Or do I withdraw?

    d) How do I deal with negative feelings?

    e) How do I deal with feelings of rage and anger?

22. a) How do I normally settle arguments?

    b) How vocal am I during arguments?

    c) How do I rate my listening skills?

d) Do I ever use the "silent treatment" to get my way? Yes / No. If yes: under what conditions?

e) Do I use hurting sarcasm? Yes / No. If yes: under what conditions?

f) How often am I willing to give in?

g) How often do I say things that I wish I could take back?

h) Am I a good loser or do I hold a grudge?

i) Do I fight fair? All the time? Sometimes? Seldom?

23. a) Do I ever solve difficulties with violence? Yes / No.

b) Under what conditions?

24. How much "private time" do I normally need?

LOVE & SEX:

1. Do I believe in pre-marital intercourse? Yes / No.
2. Have I ever had sexual problems? Yes / No. Explain:
3. a) How often would I like to have intercourse?
   b) How long does it take me to become aroused and how is this accomplished?
   c) How long should love-making last?
   d) How experimental would I like to be?
   e) Where do I NOT like to be touched?

GENERAL:

1. Do we come from the same:

    a) Cultural background? Yes / No.

    b) Educational background? Yes / No.

    c) Religious background? Yes / No.

2. What adjustments will we have to make so we can live in harmony?

3. Do I feel we should live together before we marry? Yes / No.

4. How long should we know each other before we marry?

5. What do I hope marriage will offer me, that I don't have now?

6. Why do I want to get married?

7. a) What is my view of marriage commitment?

    b) Do I believe in remaining faithful? Yes / No. Even when situations aren't going well? Yes / No.

    c) What would I do if he had an affair with someone else?

8. Which of my outside interests and work will I **NOT** share with him?

9. a) What kind of job do I (will I) have?

    b) Do I have a good job track record (stable history)? Yes / No. Explain:

    c) Will I travel with my job? Yes / No.

    d) If so, how much?

e) How would I feel if I made more money than my husband? (Be honest!)

f) Might we have to move for future job prospects? Yes / No.

g) How would I react if my company asked me to move to another city?

h) How do I think **HE** would react if my company wanted me to move to another city?

10. How would I feel if he had to return to school for several years and I was the sole breadwinner?

11. Do I have a will? Yes / No. Am I willing to prepare one as soon as we get married? Yes / No.

12. Do I have any life insurance? Yes / No. Should we get some? Yes / No. How much?

13. Should we keep liquor in our home? Yes / No. Why?

14. a) What religion will we follow (if any)?

b) How much time, energy and effort will this involve?

c) What religion will our children follow?

15. a) How often would we go on holidays?

b) How and where would we spend them?

16. a) What is it that attracts me to him?

b) Which of his qualities do I think he should change or improve?

c) What qualities of mine do I hope to change or improve?

17. a) If he suddenly became paralysed or disfigured, how would I react?

   b) If I died first, would I expect him to remarry? Yes / No. Explain:

   c) If he died first, would I expect to remarry? Yes / No. Explain:

18. Anything your fiancé should know about you, your past, your future?

SECOND MARRIAGES:

1. a) Will we be signing a pre-nuptial agreement? Yes /
   No.

   b) If so, when and what would it include?

2. What caused my earlier marriage(s) to fail? Explain:

3. If I have children from an earlier marriage:

   a) What custody arrangements are in place?

   b) What part does my ex-husband play in the
   upbringing of my children?

c) What part does my ex-husband's family (my children's grandparents, aunts, uncles, cousins) play in our lives?

d) How do they view my re-marriage plans? My fiancé? Any problems?

e) How does my fiancé get along with my children?

f) How do I feel about his parenting and disciplining abilities?

g) Will I want him to parent and discipline my children? Yes / No.

h) What will my children call him?

4. a) If he has children from an earlier marriage, how do I get along with his children?

b) Will his children be living with us? Full time? Part-time?

c) How do I feel about parenting and disciplining his children?

d) What part does his ex-wife play in his children's lives?

e) What part will his ex-wife's family (his children's grandparents, aunts, uncles, cousins) play in our lives?

f) Do I realise that if his ex-wife dies that I may become his children's full-time step-parent? Yes / No.

5. a) Any potential problems with any of our children? Yes / No. Explain:

b) Will counselling be necessary? Yes / No.

c) If yes, when will counselling happen and who will arrange it?

6. Will we live in his home? My home? Find another?

7. What part will our children play in our marriage ceremony?

***

Now - make an appointment with him so you can discuss your two sets of answers. You'll find that there are many areas where you don't think alike. That's okay - no two people can agree on everything. However, it's important that you identify the areas that might cause you problems after you're married. Be ready to make compromises where necessary.

Best wishes for a successful wedding and a long and happy marriage!

CHAPTER 2

PRE-MARITAL QUESTIONS

HIS

Answer the following questions when you have time to really consider what you want to answer. Do **NOT** complete your questions together, otherwise you will influence each other's answers.

Be sure to complete these questions **BEFORE** getting married:

IS IT "TRUE LOVE?"

There are many signs that point to true love. Here are some of them - decide what you would answer. Just put a **tick mark** next to those you agree with, and an **"X"** next to the ones you don't agree with.

1. When I consider the person I'd prefer be with - it's with her.
2. I find I've quit examining and sizing up other women as potential mates.
3. I'm quite content with her as she is. I wouldn't change any of her major characteristics.
4. I respect her talents and abilities.
5. She doesn't try to change how I am or things I believe in.
6. I find her to be a very interesting person.
7. I respect and trust her.
8. I feel we could be best friends for life.
9. This is the strongest relationship in my life.
10. I miss her when we're not together.

11. I always think of her - she's always present with me wherever I go, if only in spirit.

12. I feel excitement when we're together.

13. I have a special feeling about her that I don't feel with anyone else.

14. We don't have to talk to be companionable.

15. We both want to surprise each other with little things we know will please the other.

16. We have a strong physical attraction, love touching, and ache for each other when we're apart.

17. When we're together, I'm the happiest I can remember.

18. We love planning activities we can do together.

19. We're very protective of the other's well-being and are ready to defend each other.

20. We have a great deal of influence over each other.

21. We're on the same wave-length and often know what the other is thinking.

22. I would never deceive or be unfaithful to her.

23. We like each other's friends.

24. We enjoy doing many of the same activities.

25. We feel we could grow old happily with each other.

26. We're capable of being very intimate – there are no barriers between us. We're freely able to tell each other how we feel and discuss situations that bother us.

27. I feel she had good role models. If she didn't, she's had counselling to make sure the cycle doesn't repeat itself.

28. We're not afraid to be vulnerable to each other. We trust each other not to hurt the other.

29. We're not together simply because we don't want to be alone.

30. We both want a partner, not because we need one, but because we want one.

31. We are fulfilled, and happy with ourselves as people.

32. We're there to help celebrate each other's good days and cheer and support each other through bad days.

33. We stand by each other when we're sick, depressed or vulnerable to others.

34. We encourage each other to have other lives with our families and friends.

35. We are not possessive or jealous when we're in mixed company. Our trust for each other allows us to know the other will do the right thing.

36. We do not depend on each other to give each other a good day - we're able to do that for ourselves.

37. There are no topics or issues we can't or won't discuss.

PRE-MARITAL QUESTIONS

Now that you've established that you **are** in love, answer the following as honestly as possible. Take your time to seriously consider each question:

OUR WEDDING

1. a) What kind of wedding will we have - large small, house of worship, celebrant, Justice of the Peace?

   b) What kind of service will we have?

   c) Who will be paying for which marriage expenses?

   d) Where will we hold our wedding (what city, town, which house of worship)?

   e) Where will the reception be held?

   f) How many people will we invite? Young children too?

g) Will we both invite an equal number of guests? Yes / No.

h) If parents divorced - any problems anticipated? Describe:

i) Who will stand up for us? Her? Me?

j) Who will give her away?

k) Where and how will we spend our honeymoon?

l) Will we have an engagement party? Yes / No.

m) Do an engagement announcement? Yes / No.

n) What will our wedding invitations say?

2. a) Will she be keeping her maiden name, or will she use my name?

b) At home? At work?

AT HOME:

1. a) Where will we live: in an apartment, home, with family?

   b) Which city or town?

2. a) What major possessions will I bring into our home?

   b) What items do I feel we need to buy for our home?

   c) How much money will we need for this?

3. Do I have a car? Yes / No. How much is owing on it?

4. Should we both have an equal say in all family decisions? Yes / No. Explain:

5. How much housework would each of us do? She? Me?

6. a) How often do I like to eat out?

   b) Do I like to cook? Yes / No.

   c) What are my favourite foods?

   d) What foods do I hate/won't eat?

7. Do I like pets? Do I expect to have one or more in my home? Explain:

CHILDREN:

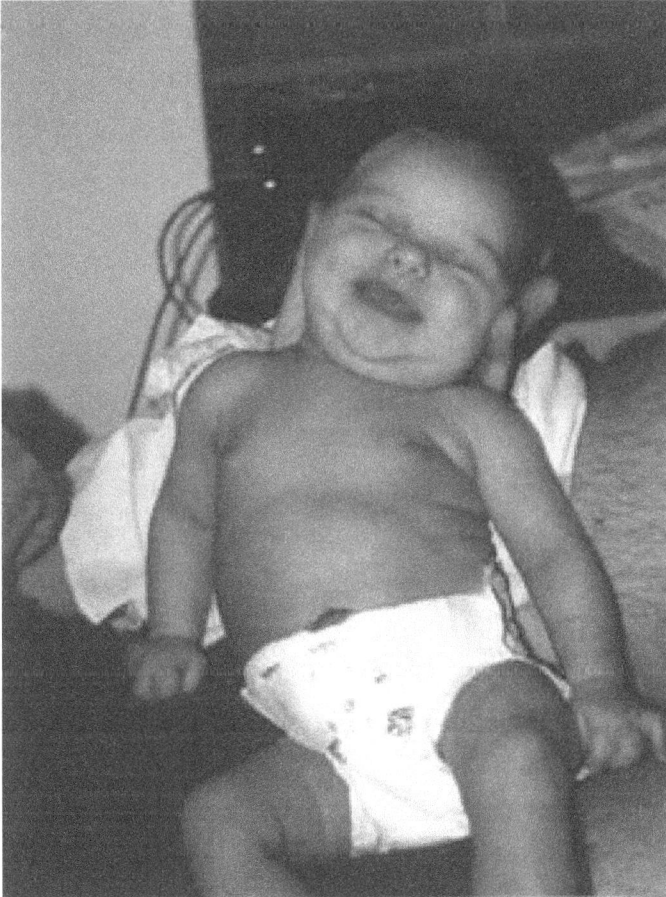

1. Am I able to father children? If not, why not?

2.a) How do I feel about mothers working after they have children?

   b) If they stay at home - for how long?

3. a) What are my views on birth control?

   b) What method of birth control would I want to use?

   c) What are my views on abortion?

d) Have I ever fathered a child who was aborted? Yes / No. If yes, explain:

4. a) How many children do I want? Boys? Girls?

   b) When would I like to start a family?

   c) If a child were to arrive before that time, how would I feel?

   d) If our child was born with a deformity, a disability or mentally challenged would I accept the child? Yes / No.

   e) Would I love this child less? Yes / No.

   f) What if we couldn't have our own children, would I want to adopt? Yes / No.

   g) Of our own culture? Other?

   h) Would I treat an adopted child as if it were mine? Yes / No.

5. a) How much time am I willing to give to the actual upbringing of our children?

   b) Would I be willing to get up at night to care for our children?

   c) What duties would I **NOT** be willing to do for our children?

6. a) Describe what I think my parenting style would be.

   b) Who should discipline our children? She? Me? Both?

FINANCES:

1. How much money will we have to live on. Her salary? Mine?

2. Would I describe myself as: Frugal? Spend freely?

3. How do I spend my money?

4. What percentage/amount of our budget should we spend on fun?

5. a) Name the credit cards I use regularly:

   b) What amount of money do I owe now (credit cards, loans, etc)? Give details on repayment arrangements.

   c) How do I use my credit cards now?

   d) How will I use credit in the future?

6. a) Will we keep a budget? Yes / No.

   b) Do I know how to keep a budget? Yes / No.

c) Who will manage our money? I manage? She manage? We'll manage together? How will we do this?

7. a) How do I feel we should handle our paycheques and bills?

b) Should we have: Joint? Separate? or both? Bank accounts?

c) How much money will each of us have to spend on ourselves each week? She? Me? Who will decide this?

MY HISTORY:

1. Have I been married before? Explain.

2. a) Have I ever had children? Explain.

   b) What part will they play in our lives?

3. a) Do I have any disabilities she doesn't know about? Yes / No. If yes: explain:

   b) Do I take medication for any chronic illness? Yes / No. If yes: explain:

   c) Do I snore? Yes / No.

   d) How is my general health? Physical? Emotional? Mental? Explain:

   e) Do I like to be busy? Prefer a less-hectic lifestyle?

4. Do I have an under- or overweight problem? Yes / No.

5. a) How do I get along with my parents?

   b) My brothers?

   c) My sisters?

   d) Other relatives?

   e) Explain:

6. How often would we visit my family – they visit us? Explain:

7. What kind of childhood did I have? Explain:

8. a) Did I come from a dysfunctional home? Explain.

   b) If so, did I obtain counselling? Yes / No.

9. Have I ever had a criminal record? Yes / No. Explain:

10. Do I like to gamble? Yes / No. If excessive, explain:

11. Amount of alcohol consumed in a week? Explain: Any drug dependency? Explain:

12. What are my views on: Having guns in our home? Capital punishment?

13. a) What is my driving record? Explain if there have been difficulties:

   b) Do I ever drink and drive or drive unsafely? Yes / No.

14. Am I going to continue smoking (if applicable)? Yes / No.

15. Will we allow smoking in our home or vehicles? Yes / No.

MY PERSONALITY:

1. Am I a: neat? messy? person?

2. Am I a: morning? night? person?

3. Describe my average energy level - High? Medium? Low?

4. How do I manage time? Always early? Late? Procrastinate?

5. Am I a pack-rat? Dispose of unnecessary clutter?

6. Do I like to pull practical jokes? Have I hurt others' feelings?

7. Do I feel comfortable discussing my innermost feelings? Yes / No. Explain:

8. How important to me is the expression of affection? Explain:

9. Am I a romantic person (flowers, love notes, etc.)? Yes / No.

10. Do I like to be touched? Yes / No. In public? Only where there's privacy?

11. Do I prefer: being with friends? being alone? with family members?

12. How often would I like to entertain? Explain: Her friends: My friends:

13. Do I dislike any of her friends? Yes / No. Explain:

14. a) How do I view her having friends of the opposite sex?

    b) Would I object if she saw other men alone? Yes / No.

c) Would I describe myself as a jealous person? Yes / No.

d) If yes, how do I deal with jealousy?

15. When we're married, how much time will I spend with "the boys?"

16. How do I like to spend my leisure time?

17. How much time do I spend on hobbies or volunteer work?

18. Would I describe myself as a workaholic? Yes / No. Explain:

19. a) Describe my basic personality type: Extrovert? Introvert?

   b) Do I like to have music or the radio playing? Or do I like it best when it's quiet?

20. a) Do I feel comfortable giving/receiving compliments? Yes / No.

   b) Do I need reassurance from the important people in my life? Yes? Sometimes? No.

21. a) Describe my moods - steady, erratic, up one minute – down the next?

   b) How do I deal with and relieve stress? Explain:

   c) When I'm troubled, do I share my problems? Or do I withdraw?

   d) How do I deal with negative feelings?

   e) How do I deal with feelings of rage and anger?

22. a) How do I normally settle arguments?

   b) How vocal am I during arguments?

   c) How do I rate my listening skills?

d) Do I ever use the "silent treatment" to get my way? Yes / No. If yes: under what conditions?

e) Do I use hurting sarcasm? Yes / No. If yes: under what conditions?

f) How often am I willing to give in?

g) How often do I say things that I wish I could take back?

h) Am I a good loser or do I hold a grudge?

i) Do I fight fair? All the time? Sometimes? Seldom?

23. a) Do I ever solve difficulties with violence? Yes / No.

b) Under what conditions?

24. How much "private time" do I normally need?

LOVE & SEX:

1. Do I believe in pre-marital intercourse? Yes / No.

2. Have I ever had sexual problems? Yes / No. Explain:

3. a) How often would I like to have intercourse?

   b) How long does it take me to become aroused and how is this accomplished?

   c) How long should love-making last?

   d) How experimental would I like to be?

   e) Where do I NOT like to be touched?

GENERAL

1. Do we come from the same:

   a) Cultural background? Yes / No.

   b) Educational background? Yes / No.

   c) Religious background? Yes / No.

2. What adjustments will we have to make so we can live in harmony?

3. Do I feel we should live together before we marry? Yes / No.

4. How long should we know each other before we marry?

5. What do I hope marriage will offer me, that I don't have now?

6. Why do I want to get married?

7. a) What is my view of marriage commitment?

   b) Do I believe in remaining faithful? Yes / No. Even when situations aren't going well? Yes / No.

   c) What would I do if she had an affair with someone else?

8. Which of my outside interests and work will I **NOT** share with her?

9. a) What kind of job do I (will I) have?

   b) Do I have a good job track record (stable history)? Yes / No. Explain:

   c) Will I travel with my job? Yes / No.

   d) If so, how much?

e) How would I feel if my wife made more money than me? (Be honest!)

f) Might we have to move for future job prospects? Yes / No.

g) How would I react if my company asked me to move to another city?

h) How do I think **SHE** would react if my company wanted me to move to another city?

10. How would I feel if she had to return to school for several years and I was the sole breadwinner?

11. Do I have a will? Yes / No. Am I willing to prepare one as soon as we get married? Yes / No.

12. Do I have any life insurance? Yes / No. Should we get some? Yes / No. How much?

13. Should we keep liquor in our home? Yes / No. Why?

14. a) What religion will we follow (if any)?

b) How much time, energy and effort will this involve?

c) What religion will our children follow?

15. a) How often would we go on holidays?

b) How and where would we spend them?

16. a) What is it that attracts me to her?

b) Which of her qualities do I think she should change or improve?

c) What qualities of mine do I hope to change or improve?

17. a) If she suddenly became paralysed or disfigured, how would I react?

b) If I died first, would I expect her to remarry? Yes / No. Explain:

c) If she died first, would I expect to remarry? Yes / No. Explain:

18. Anything your fiancé should know about you, your past, your future?

SECOND MARRIAGES:

1. a) Will we be signing a pre-nuptial agreement? Yes /
      No.

   b) If so, when, and what would it include?

2. What caused my earlier marriage(s) to fail? Explain:

3. If I have children from an earlier marriage:

   a) What custody arrangements are in place?

   b) What part does my ex-wife play in the upbringing of
      my children?

c) What part does my ex-wife's family (my children's grandparents, aunts, uncles, cousins) play in our lives?

d) How do they view my re-marriage plans? My fiancé? Any problems?

e) How does my fiancé get along with my children?

f) How do I feel about her parenting and disciplining abilities?

g) Will I want her to parent and discipline my children? Yes / No.

h) What will my children call her?

4. a) If she has children from an earlier marriage, how do I get along with her children?

b) Will her children be living with us? Full time? Part-time?

c) How do I feel about parenting and disciplining her children?

d) What part does her ex-husband play in her children's lives?

e) What part will her ex-husband's family (her children's grandparents, aunts, uncles, cousins) play in our lives?

f) Do I realise that if her ex-husband dies that I may become her children's full-time step-parent? Yes / No.

5. a) Any potential problems with any of our children? Yes / No. Explain:

b) Will counselling be necessary? Yes / No.

c) If yes, when will counselling happen and who will arrange it?

6. Will we live in her home? My home? Find another?

7. What part will our children play in our marriage ceremony?

***

Now - make an appointment with him so you can discuss your two sets of answers. You'll find that there are many areas where you don't think alike. That's okay - no two people can agree on everything. However, it's important that you identify the areas that might cause you problems after you're married. Be ready to make compromises where necessary.

Best wishes for a successful wedding and a long and happy marriage!

CHAPTER 3

WEDDING TIPS

BRIDE'S "TO DO" LIST

One Year Before the Wedding:

- Discuss the wedding budget with both sets of parents. Decide who's paying for what.
- Choose your wedding date (have a second choice in mind). Arrange to meet with the clergy member who will perform the ceremony.
- Make reception reservations - hall, menu, catering, music, bartenders, wine list.

- Choose matron of honour, bridesmaids, flower girl, and advise them of their roles.
- Arrange for the soloist, organist or other musicians.
- Place engagement announcement in newspaper.

Six Months Before the Wedding:

- Select your wedding gown, veil, headpiece, shoes and garter. Make sure shoes are well broken in.
- Choose and book photographer and/or videographer.
- Arrange for limousine or other transportation.
- Start guest list and notify your fiance's family to do the same.
- Choose your attendants' and flower girl dresses.
- Register for china, crystal, flatware, linens and other gifts.
- Discuss honeymoon plans, send away for brochures, visit travel agent.
- Decide where you will live after your marriage.

Four Months Before the Wedding:

- Help groom choose his tuxedo.
- Complete guest list.
- Arrange honeymoon and get vaccinations.
- Renew your passport if necessary and obtain required visas.

- Order invitations and other stationary (don't forget guest book).
- Order flowers - plan altar/reception arrangements.
- Meet with the musicians to select music.
- Rent punchbowls and accessories.
- Shop for wedding bands.
- Shop for trousseau and lingerie.
- Establish gift register.

Two Months Before the Wedding:

- Order wedding cake.
- Finalise reception menu.
- Choose trousseau and going-away outfits.
- Have make-up and hair consultations.
- Address invitations and announcements.
- Mail invitations to arrive six weeks before the wedding.
- Attend fittings for gown and make appointments for attendants' fittings.
- Arrange name change documents (bank, charge and credit cards etc.)
- Arrange where attendants will dress for wedding.
- Prepare place cards for seating of guests.
- Set rehearsal date.

One Month Before the Wedding:

- Have final dress fitting.
- Book hairdresser and cosmetician for wedding day.
- Buy groom's and attendants' gifts.
- Write thank-you notes as gifts are received.
- Arrange accommodations for out-of-town guests.
- Confirm details - hall, caterer, liquor, florist, photographer, musicians, etc.
- Be prepared to attend bridal showers.
- Practice wedding waltz.
- Engrave wedding rings.
- Write vows and inform celebrant.
- Ask yourself - are you doing the right thing by marrying this man?

Two Weeks Before the Wedding:

- Review all transportation arrangements to the church.
- Continue with "thank-you" notes.
- Pick up wedding cake and make preparations for wedding cake distribution.
- Arrange who will return hire items.
- Buy travellers' checks for honeymoon.
- Collect purchases such as rings, gifts, accessories.

One Week Before the Wedding:

- Be sure to confirm times and final details with:
    - caterer
    - florist
    - photographer
    - band, musicians
    - limousine company
    - any other suppliers
- Give gifts to your attendants.
- Pick up your wedding gown.
- Arrange for wedding announcement for newspaper.
- Pack for honeymoon.
- Pick up flowers.
- Pick up wedding rings.
- Attend wedding rehearsal.
- Remain calm!

On the BIG Day:

- Get hair and makeup done.
- Review with your matron of honour, brides maids, and flower girl their obligations and timing for the day.
- Ensure you have his wedding ring - give it to your matron of honour or ring bearer.
- Have matron of honour bring guest book and guest list for reception.

- Arrive at the church early enough to check your hair, makeup and wedding attire.
- Marriage ceremony.
- Attend wedding reception.
- Dance wedding waltz with new husband.
- Cut and distribute wedding cake.
- Have fun!
- Throw bridal bouquet.
- Go on honeymoon.

GROOM'S "TO DO" LIST

Six Months - One Year Before the Wedding:

- Arrange a visit with the clergy to set the date and time of the ceremony.

- Choose your best man/master of ceremonies, ushers and ring bearer and advise them of their roles.

- Book hall, catering, liquor, bartenders and music.

- Choose photographer and/or videographer.
- With both sets of parents, establish a budget, financial responsibilities and guest list.
- Buy engagement ring and choose wedding bands.
- Decide where you'll live after your marriage.

Three Months Before the Wedding:

- Obtain marriage licence.
- Order wedding attire for yourself and your attendants and purchase your going away suit and accessories.
- Complete your family's guest list.
- Order limousines - ask if deposit is necessary.
- Buy gifts for your bride, best man, ushers and ring bearer.
- Make honeymoon arrangements; visa, passport and inoculations for both bride and groom.
- Confirm accommodations for wedding night.

One Month Before the Wedding

- Arrange overnight accommodations for out-of-town guests.
- Schedule a rehearsal for the week prior to thewedding.
- Assist with plans for rehearsal dinner.
- Practice wedding waltz.
- Engrave wedding rings.

- Write vows for wedding and inform celebrant.
- Order liquor for wedding rehearsal party.
- Arrange tuxedo fittings.
- Confirm honeymoon reservations and buy travellers' cheques.
- Ask yourself if you are doing the right thing marrying this woman.

One Week Before the Wedding:

- Pick up your wedding attire.
- Pick up wedding bands.
- Advise your best man and ushers regarding the rehearsal and any special arrangements for the service.
- Give gifts to your attendants.
- Prepare your toast to the bride speech.
- Review procedures with master of ceremonies.
- Pick up reservations for honeymoon, wedding night etc.
- Attend rehearsal.
- Pack for honeymoon.
- Decorate wedding cars.

On the BIG Day:

- Ensure the best man has the honorarium for the clergy, caretaker, organist, soloist, and cheques for the band, caterers etc.

- Review with your best man, ushers, ring bearer their obligations and timing for the day.
- Give wedding band(s) to best man.
- Arrive at the church 20 minutes before ceremony.
- Marriage ceremony.
- Attend wedding reception.
- Make toast to the bride.
- Cut and distribute wedding cake.
- Dance wedding waltz with new bride.
- Remove and throw bride's garter.
- Have fun!
- Go on honeymoon.

Best man's duties:

- Stand up for the Groom.
- Master of Ceremonies.
- Introduce head table at reception.
- Initiate toasts.
- Make announcements as required.
- Ensure that payments are made for services rendered.

TIPS FOR CHOOSING

THE PERFECT WEDDING GOWN

Bridal salons have seen it all:

- brides in tears because the gown's alterations weren't done,
- panicked because their gown arrived at the last minute,
- distraught because she wanted an imported gown in three weeks and found that it would take months,
- mortified because she gained or lost weight and the gown didn't fit.

Tips that can eliminate disaster:

1. Choose a full service bridal salon where its staff has the specific experience required for this very specialised sale.
2. Start a file and collect ideas long before you set out to visit a bridal salon.
3. Buy bridal magazines to get an overview of what's available. Most magazines give you style numbers and telephone numbers so you can make inquiries.
4. Remember that American and European magazines show gowns that are probably not available in other countries.
5. Regular ordering should take eight to ten weeks. If gown has to be custom made, allow at least four to six months after you place your order.
6. If you don't usually have clothes made by a dressmaker, beware of having a bridal gown made by a dressmaker. Most of us can't visualise a style as it will look on our figures.

82

7. Take the pictures you've chosen to the salon. These will give your consultant an overview of your preferences.

8. Work with a consultant you feel comfortable with. If you don't feel good vibes, ask for someone else.

9. Try on various styles of gowns. You may be surprised at what looks good on you.

10. It's confusing to visit too many boutiques. Narrow your choices down to two or three.

11. Make notes after each visit to a salon. Keep record of prices, styles, delivery time, accessories offered, and more. Ask if the store has a lay-away plan.

12. Don't comparison shop by phone. Price alone shouldn't be the bottom line.

13. Bring along only one person to advise you Too many influences will confuse you.

Don't dress to please anyone else.

14. Beware that white doesn't always mean white - it depends on the type of fabric. Silk, for example, is usually eggshell. On the other hand, most satins are very white. Some have yellow or pink sheens.

15. Inquire about the store's policy on custom-fittings. Ask about and be prepared to pay additional cost for the alterations. Most full-service bridal boutiques have fully qualified seamstresses available.

Obtain written estimates.

16. At the fitting, wear the shoes with the exact heel as those you will wear on your wedding day. Also, wear the appropriate undergarments for your style of gown.

17. Be prepared to pay a deposit of at least fifty percent of the cost on your gown at the time you place your order. Larger sizes may be subject to fifteen to twenty-five percent surcharge - but remember that this surcharge is imposed by the manufacturer - not the boutique.

18. Don't let the offer of a free gift influence your final choice of boutique. A gift is lovely, if everything else is equal, but don't overlook boutiques that offer a full range of styles, experienced personnel and a good reputation.

19. Don't arrive with lots of friends for your final fitting.

20. Be prepared to pay the balance owing on your gown upon its delivery. You can arrange monthly payments if you like, so that the final payment will coincide with the delivery of your gown. See that financial arrangements are clear and in writing.

WEDDING BUDGET CHECK LIST

Ceremony costs:

Marriage licence

Clergy's honorarium

Organist/Soloist

Decorations/Cushions

Caretaker

Gifts:

Bride to groom

Groom to bride

Attendants

Photography:

Photographer

Videographer.

Personal Effects

Wedding dress/shoes

Veil and headpiece

Jewellery

Garter

Going away outfits

Shoes and accessories

Lingerie

Groom's tuxedo/shoes

Hairdresser, barber

Gown and tuxedo cleaning

Wedding/engagement rings.

Transportation & Accommodation

Hotel accommodation, wedding night and honeymoon.

Limousine/car rental

Flight costs for honeymoon

Vehicle decoration

Stationery

Invitations

Announcements

Thank-you notes

Reply cards

Guest mementoes

Newspaper announcements

Matches/serviettes

Guest book

Stamps

Reception

Hall rental

Meals

Liquor license

Wine and liquor

Bartender

Gratuities

Punch glass rental

Music

Equipment hire

Miscellaneous

Insurance

Flowers

Bride's bouquet

Corsages

Bridesmaids' bouquets

Boutonnieres
- going away
- mothers'
- step-mothers'
- grandmothers'
- flower girl
- ring bearer

Alter arrangements

Bride's home

Reception

Wedding Cake

Kitchen piece (for guests to take home)

Cake knife

Cutting and wrapping

Wedding cake boxes

WHO PAYS FOR WHAT?

The Bride
Groom's ring

Gift for groom

Gifts for bridesmaids

Stationery – thank-you notes

Accommodations for out-of-town bridesmaids

The Groom
Bride's rings

Gift for bride

Gifts for best man, ushers, ring bearer

Marriage licence

Accommodations for out-of-town ushers and/or best man

Bride's bouquet, going-away corsage

Bridesmaids' flowers, corsage for mothers and boutonnieres for men in wedding party

Celebrant's fee

Bachelor party

Honeymoon

Bride's Family:
Engagement party

Wedding reception costs (food, hall, decorations, drinks, entertainment, cake, flowers and gratuities)

Gift for newlyweds

Announcements, invitations and postage

Bridal outfits

Photographer

Limo to ceremony, reception, parking/valet charges

Groom's Family:

Groom's wedding clothes

Gift for newlyweds

Rehearsal dinner

Bride or Groom's Family:

Ceremony costs, music and decorations of hall

Bridesmaids flowers

Attendants:

Wedding outfits and accessories

Travelling expenses and accommodation

Gift for newlyweds.

WEDDING TOASTS

Bridegroom to bride:

"The best is yet to be."

"Grow old with me."

"Walk by my side forever."

Bride to groom:

"May we protect and cherish each other forever."

"Never above you. Never below you. Always beside you."

Parents to bride and groom:

"From this day forward, here's to your health and happiness."

"To new beginnings."

"To the successful joining of two families."

91

To guests:

"May the friends of our youth be the companions of our old age."

"Our home will always welcome you."

"To those who took the time to celebrate this special day with us."

Second marriage toast:

"Here's to a second chance at happiness."

"To the successful joining of two families."

DRESS CODE – WOMEN

White Tie

Also referred to as full evening dress or evening dress – this is the most formal of all t5he dress codes. White tie calls for a full-length, formal evening dress. Shorter dresses or trousers for women are considered unacceptable. Extravagant jewellery may be work to complement the gown and evening bags would be small and elegant. Shoes should have a high heel.

Black Tie

Slightly less dressy than the white tie code but generally requires a floor-length gown in any colour. Dressy trousers, preferably in a wider cut are acceptable with fine jewellery and an elegant evening bag. Hair can be styled in an up-do or may be worn down. Shoes would have a medium to high heel.

Cocktail

Cocktail dresses are slightly dressier than a lounge suit or can be a knee-length or mid-length dress. Most are darker or richer in colour and fabric and may have sequins or beading. Worn with high heels, dressy jewellery and small evening bag.

Lounge Suit

Can be a knee-length dress in a light colour and fabric, leaning more towards a day dress worn with mid to high heels and understated jewellery. A more casual bag or oversized clutch is acceptable.

Smart Casual

Is the most confusing of all dress codes, but you are encouraged to dress appropriately for the event you attend. A blouse and skirt, jumpsuit or well-cut trousers or tailored shorts with silk camisole top and heels would be acceptable. Simple jewellery and an understated shoulder bag. Denim jeans or shorts should be avoided unless it is for a barbecue or informal gathering.

DRESS CODE – MEN

White Tie

Also referred to as full evening dress, full dress or evening dress – this is the most formal of all the dress codes. For men, white tie calls for full coat and tails, black tailcoat worn over a white starched shirt, Marcella waistcoat and a white bow tie worn around a detachable collar. Accessorise with cufflinks and shirt studs.

Black Tie

Slightly less dressy than the white tie code – requires a tuxedo and white dinner shirt and black bow tie. Accessorise with freshly polished patent leather shoes with long black socks and a white handkerchief or pocket square tucked into the left breast pocket of the jacket.

Cocktail

A tailored, slim cut charcoal or black suit with a white shirt and patterned tie and ensure shoes are freshly polished.

Lounge Suit

This is an every-day business suit. You can be a bit more creative with colour – wearing navy, blue, grey or taupe suit paired with a patterned or coloured shirt with a tie and pocket square.

Smart Casual

Pair a blazer or sports coat with slacks or chinos with a collared shirt – preferably in a lighter colour. No tie required and if it's hot ditch the jacket. Shirt needs to be freshly pressed and tucked into pants. Denim is avoided and shorts are a no-no.

MARRIAGE CONTRACTS

PRE-NUPTIAL AGREEMENTS

Before preparing a cohabitation, marriage or pre-nuptial agreement, make sure you check the laws in your area. Every province, state and country has their own laws. I've quoted from the laws in Canada.

Most couples who request marriage contracts do so with the idea of making some provision for their property that differs from that set out in the Family Law Act. In Ontario (most provinces are similar) there are four possible approaches to the division of property; separate property regime, some kind of community property regime, a Family Law Reform Act regime, or a modified Family Law Reform Act regime.

A husband and wife looking to devise a personal property regime of their own should become acquainted with each system - their advantages and disadvantages. They'll need to establish:

a) How they will hold their marital property during their marriage.

b) Which property should be shared upon a marriage breakdown.

Separate Property Arrangements:

Property brought into the marriage by a spouse remains the separate property of the spouse who acquired it or in whose name it is held (with the exception of property transferred from a wife to a husband where the presumption of resulting trust arises). Spouses may dispose of their assets during marriage as they wish, with no restraint.

A professional couple with no children, with equal incomes and a desire to remain independent may balk at the sharing provisions of the Family Law Act; as might an older couple in a second marriage who perhaps have substantial assets and wish to maintain their property separately.

Their marriage contract would set out a separate property regime that states that neither party shall have a claim of any kind against property owned by the other under any current or future legislation. There should also be a statement that no property in which either party has or may acquire an interest shall be included in his or her net family property, and that each party shall always have a net family property of zero.

If each party is to keep the property s/he owns, it will be vital to be able to prove ownership. The contract should clearly spell out the way in which ownership will be decided (registered titles, cancelled cheques, credit card receipts etc.)

Community Property Regime:

Combines the property and assets of the couple into a unified "community" instead of distinguishing between "his" and "hers." Community property is "theirs." Each spouse owns half of the property based on the assumption that both spouses have contributed equally to the economic assets of the marriage whether by assuming household management and child care responsibilities or by earning income outside the home.

The traditional community property regime gives the husband the power to manage the joint assets during marriage. Most modern Canadian couples find this unacceptable. The more acceptable regime emphasises the concept that a marriage is a joint venture. A couple who wish a truly egalitarian marriage may find that only the full and immediate community property regime is acceptable. For a spouse not employed outside the home, such an arrangement would also provide emotional and psychological benefits derived from the reality of present, not deferred, ownership. This redresses the financial imbalance between some spouses during their marriage, as well as show a clear signal to the unemployed spouse that his or her assumption of household management and child-raising responsibilities is valued.

When two individuals manage one piece of property, neither one has veto power over the other. One problem arises when community funds are used to pay off debts on or to improve one spouse's separate property. Other difficulties may arise where separate property has been used to improve, or discharge debts on community property. Upon dissolution of a marriage, this can affect not only the spouses themselves, but their respective heirs and beneficiaries, creditors or taxing authorities. The concept of equality that is the foundation of the regime is attained through a complex set of regulations governing both spouses and all the persons with whom they interact.

In choosing between a deferred community of property regime, and a full and immediate one with joint management, the trade-offs must be careful considered. As a deferred community regime is much less complex, spouses may prefer some variation of this system, but perhaps not exactly the one set out in the Family Law Act.

Family Law Reform Act Regime:

Some couples believe that the property regime set out under the Family Law Reform Act is preferable to the new provisions of the Family Law Act. They feel that the distinction between "family assets" and "non-family assets" is a valid one. There is nothing to prevent those couples from stipulating that their family assets will be divided equally, while their non-family assets will remain the property of the person who owns them.

It would be wise in any marriage contract that adopts the Family Law Reform Act regime, to define the terms and to list the specific assets that fall into each category when drafting the contract.

This regime suits a couple where both parties have substantial investments they wish to protect, or where one spouse wishes to maintain a business as his or her own separate property, but is quite content to share family assets equally.

Modified Family Law Act Regime:

This might involve family heirlooms or antiques that may prove difficult to value or that the parties have agreed are to remain with one of them only upon separation. The contract could state that the value of these items would not be included in the owner spouse's net family property.

The most common situation where the parties may feel a modified Family Law Act regime is best, is where one party brings into the marriage real property that both parties use as their matrimonial home. In the absence of a marriage contract, that party would be required to include the full value of the home in his or her net family property, something both parties may agree is unfair. A marriage contract could specify the value of the home at the date of marriage and provide that only the increase in this value after marriage would be included in the owner's net family property, or alternatively, the non-owning spouse could acquire a greater interest in the home with each year of marriage.

A husband may agree that the value of his business is to be included in his net family property calculations, or a wife may agree that the increase in value of the cottage she owned at the time of the marriage and which had been in her family for years, is to be included in her net family property calculations, but both agree that the business and cottage will not be sold or encumbered to satisfy any equalisation payment owing from one to the other.

THE MATRIMONIAL HOME

The matrimonial home is often given special treatment in a marriage contract. Contrary to what many people think, it's possible to exclude the home from the owner's net family property. The prohibitions in the Family Law Act relate only to the rights of possession and disposition of the home, not ownership. If the home is owned by one spouse only, the parties might agree in a marriage contract that the property will be excluded from the owning party's net family property. In this case, the non-owning spouse should sign any documents required to permit the owner to alienate or encumber the home provided this document imposes no obligation upon the non-owner.

In the event of separation, the party who owns the home may want a provision in the contract whereby the other spouse agrees to vacate the premises upon reasonable notice from the owning spouse. Care should be taken not to offend the Family Law Act with such a provision.

Often a couple will want to own the matrimonial home together, but in unequal shares that reflect their percentage contributions in cash to the original purchase price. If they so wish, they can provide a mechanism whereby the minority owner has the right to increase his or her interest up to fifty percent by paying down the mortgage, reimbursing the majority owner for repairs, etc. If the couple are joint tenants, they may wish to specify buy-out provisions in the contract where either party would purchase the others' one-half equity.

COHABITATION AGREEMENT

Before preparing a cohabitation, marriage or pre-nuptial agreement, make sure you check the laws in your area. Every province, state and country has their own laws. I've quoted from the laws in Australia.

This agreement is made the_____day of_____20__
between

(name)_____of

Address_____

and (name)_____ of

Address_____.

RECITALS:

1. The parties entered into a defacto relationship pursuant to the Property Law Act in 1999.

2. It is the wish of the parties to fix their rights and obligations concerning their future, welfare and property, in order to promote harmony between themselves and reduce the possibility of litigation should, despite their best intentions, their relationship fail. They further wish to put their agreement to writing as to how their financial relationship should be regulated.

3. This agreement has been made by the parties pursuant to the provisions of the Property Law Act 1999 (as amended). At the time of making this agreement no other financial agreement is in force between the parties.

<u>OPERATIVE PART:</u>

Definition

1. "Parties" mean:

(name)_____

and

(name) _____

2. "Property" means the real of personal property referred to in this agreement.

3. "Relationship" means the relationship between:

(name)_____

and

(name)_____

which commenced on

(Date)_____

Assets owned by the parties prior to the relationship remain separate property

1st Person's property

1. At the commencement of the relationship,

(name) _____ owned a home **(Address)**_____

_____

Motor car **(Name make)**_____

Cash in her possession of _____together with personal items, all held in her name solely (list).

This is acknowledged by **(2nd Person's name)**

_____.

This property of **(1st Person's name),** subsequently became the current residential property at **(Address)** _____, held in **(1st Person's name)** _____ name only.

The property acquired and exchanged for or the increase in value of the separate property owned by

(1ˢᵗ Person's name) _____

as stated in this agreement will be and remain her separate property.

2ⁿᵈ Person's property

2. At the commencement of the relationship, **(2ⁿᵈ Person's name)** has no assets other than:

   Truck **(Name make)**

   _____

   Personal items (list) and _____ Cash.

Property at the option of the parties at the commencement of the relationship

3. The parties may during the relationship, jointly acquire property or interests in property, whether real or personal.

Notice of Separation

4. For the purpose of this agreement, the separation of the parties will be deemed to occur on either party sending written notice to the other party by surface mail, stating that s/he intends to terminate the relationship.

Division of property and liabilities

5. If the parties separate pursuant to the terms of this agreement the Property owned by them will be divided in accordance with their percentage of ownership as evidenced by this agreement and other written agreements signed by them.

6. Where no agreements exist, the property will be divided evenly between the parties.

7. Separate property acquired prior and subsequent to the relationship will remain separate property.

8. In the event of termination of the parties' relationship or separation of the parties, any liabilities incurred during the relationship will be divided evenly.

Amendment

This agreement may be only amended or supplemented in writing evidenced by both the parties and attached to this agreement.

Binding on Successors

This agreement is binding upon the heirs, executors and assigns of the parties.

Disclosure statement

The parties state that details of all significant property, financial resources and liabilities have been disclosed to one another and that each party is fully aware of the other party's property, financial resources and liabilities.

This document executed as a Deed

BY (name 1st Person)

_____

In the presence of:_____
Justice of the Peace/Solicitor

BY (name 2nd Person)

_____

In the presence of:_____
Justice of the Peace/Solicitor

****

You can see that these laws are complex. To learn more about your options and to seal your agreement, contact a lawyer in your area who can interpret your local laws and regulations as they relate to Marriage Contracts, Pre-Nuptial and Cohabitation Agreements.

www.ingramcontent.com/pod-product-compliance
Lightning Source LLC
LaVergne TN
LVHW041230080426
835508LV00011B/1144